★ ALL-TIME ★ BEST ATHLETES

BASKETBALL SUPERSTARS

ZELDA WAGNER

LERNER PUBLICATIONS ◆ MINNEAPOLIS

Lerner Publications Company
An imprint of Lerner Publishing Group, Inc.
241 First Avenue North
Minneapolis, MN 55401 USA

For reading levels and more information, look up this title at www.lernerbooks.com.

Main body text set in Mikado.
Typeface provided by HVD Fonts.

Image credits: Focus On Sport/Getty Images, p. 5; Icon Sportswire/Getty Images, p. 6; Focus On Sport/Getty Images Sport/Getty Images, p. 9; John W. McDonough/Sports Illustrated/Getty Images, p. 10; Ken Levine/Hulton Archive/Getty Images, p. 13; Meg Oliphant/Getty Images Sport/Getty Images, p. 14; Bettmann/Getty Images, p. 17; Steve Lipofsky/Sports Illustrated/Getty Images, p. 18; Focus On Sport/Getty Images, p. 21; Gina Ferazzi/Los Angeles Times/Getty Images, p. 23. Design element: FoxGrafy/Shutterstock; Anna Golant/Shutterstock. Cover: AP Photo/Matt York.

Designer: Kim Morales **Photo Editor:** Annie Zheng
Lerner team: Martha Kranes

Library of Congress Cataloging-in-Publication Data

Names: Wagner, Zelda, 2000- author.
Title: Basketball superstars / Zelda Wagner.
Description: Minneapolis, MN : Lerner Publications, [2025] | Series: All-time best athletes (Lerner sports rookie) | Includes bibliographical references and index. | Audience: Ages 5–8 | Audience: Grades K–1 | Summary: "Many players have raised the bar in basketball. But who played the best game? Discover the greatest players in basketball history through fun facts and incredible stats"— Provided by publisher.
Identifiers: LCCN 2023038991 (print) | LCCN 2023038992 (ebook) | ISBN 9798765625712 (library binding) | ISBN 9798765628171 (paperback) | ISBN 9798765632321 (epub)
Subjects: LCSH: Basketball players—Juvenile literature. | Basketball—Records—Juvenile literature.
Classification: LCC GV885.1 .W23 2025 (print) | LCC GV885.1 (ebook) | DDC 796.3230922—dc23/eng/20230817

LC record available at https://lccn.loc.gov/2023038991
LC ebook record available at https://lccn.loc.gov/2023038992

Manufactured in the United States of America
1-1010183-51905-11/7/2023

TABLE OF CONTENTS

Turn the pages to meet the best basketball players. Count them down from **10** to **1**. Number 1 is the best basketball player ever!

MEET THE 10 BEST BASKETBALL PLAYERS!

10. HAKEEM OLAJUWON

Hakeem Olajuwon was one of the best scorers in basketball. Players had a hard time blocking his shots.

COUNT IT!
All-Star Games: 12

4

9. MAYA MOORE

Maya Moore scored up close and far away. She led Team USA and the Minnesota Lynx to many wins.

COUNT IT!
Olympic gold medals: 2

8. LARRY BIRD

Larry Bird scored with quick shots. He often stole the ball from the other team. Then he ran down the court to score.

COUNT IT!

NBA titles: 3

7. TIM DUNCAN

Tim Duncan played in the NBA for 19 years. He blocked shots and scored a lot of points.

COUNT IT!
Points per game: 19

6. MAGIC JOHNSON

Earvin "Magic" Johnson got his nickname for his amazing skills. He passed the ball to teammates for assists.

COUNT IT!

Assists per game: 11.2

5. DIANA TAURASI

Diana Taurasi was a good shooter. She could score from anywhere on the court.

COUNT IT!
WNBA titles: 3

4. WILT CHAMBERLAIN

Wilt Chamberlain grabbed more rebounds than any other player. He led the NBA in scoring seven times!

COUNT IT!

Rebounds per game: 22.9

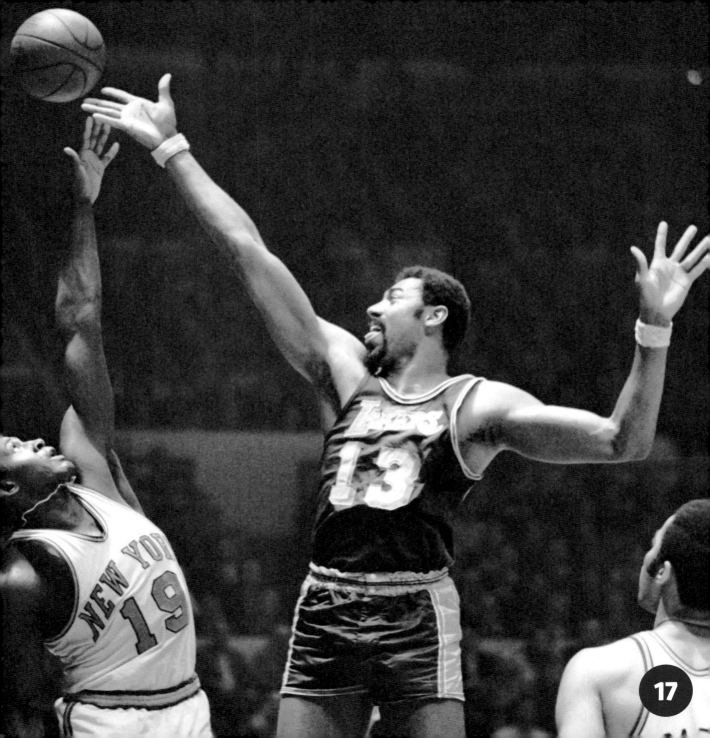

3. KAREEM ABDUL-JABBAR

Kareem Abdul-Jabbar's famous move was the skyhook shot. He could shoot over anyone blocking him.

COUNT IT!

Points per game: 24.6

19

2. MICHAEL JORDAN

Michael Jordan never gave up in a game.
He even played when he was sick. He was
a great scorer and defender.

COUNT IT!

NBA titles: 6

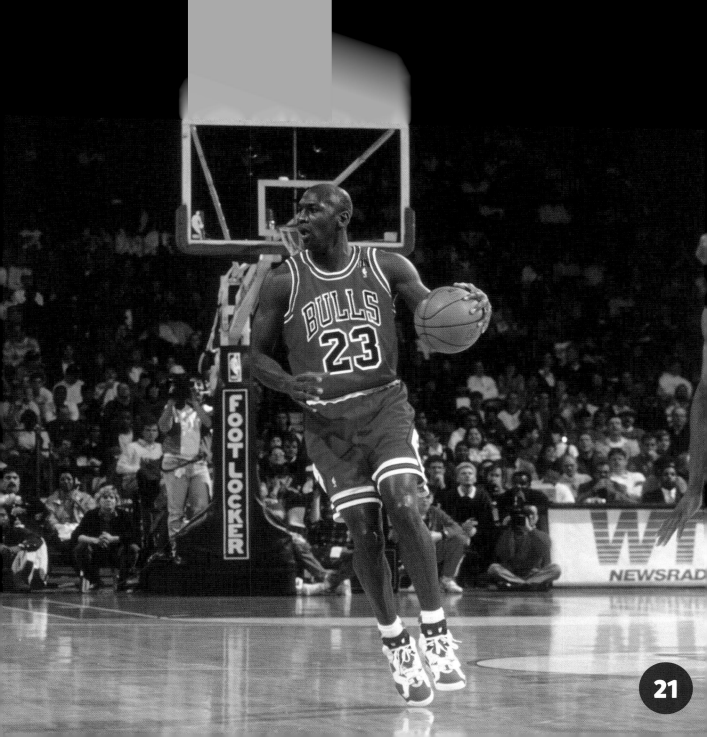

1. LEBRON JAMES

LeBron James joined the NBA just after high school. He is the NBA's all-time leading scorer.

COUNT IT!
All-Star Games: 19

NOW IT'S YOUR TURN.

Who do you think are the best basketball players? Make your own list!

GLOSSARY

assist: a pass from a teammate that leads directly to a score

NBA: short for National Basketball Association

rebound: grabbing the ball after a missed shot

title: a championship

WNBA: short for Women's National Basketball Association

LEARN MORE

Graves, Will. *NBA*. Minneapolis: Essential Library, 2021.

Leed, Percy. *Basketball: A First Look*. Minneapolis: Lerner Publications, 2023.

Rose, Rachel. *Michael Jordan: Basketball Superstar*. Minneapolis: Bearport, 2021.

INDEX